bring your racquet
tennis basics for kids

by Steven White

Author of *Teaching Tennis: Protocol for Instructors*

D1404244

Kirk House Publishers
Minneapolis, Minnesota

Bring Your Racquet

Tennis Basics for Kids

by Steven White

Library of Congress Cataloging-in-Publication Data

White, Steven, 1960-
  Bring your raquet : tennis basics for kids / by Steven White.
      p. cm.
  Includes bibliographical references and index.
  ISBN-13: 978-1-933794-24-2 (alk. paper)
  ISBN-10: 1-933794-24-0 (alk. paper)
  1. Tennis for children. 2. Tennis for children—Coaching. I. Title.
  GV1001.4.C45W55 2010
  796.342083—dc22

                              2010001566

Kirk House Publishers, PO Box 390759, Minneapolis, MN 55439
www.kirkhouse.com
Manufactured in the United States of America

table of contents

introduction

At no other time in history have so many children wanted to play tennis at such a young age. And quite naturally, young players are constantly striving to improve their games. While there are many ways to learn the game and to improve, the basics of tennis are unchanging. That is why this book, the result of over twenty-five years of tennis teaching experience, concentrates on the fundamentals of the game for the young—both the beginner and the improving player.

In this book, as a professional tennis instructor, I have illustrated the basics of the game in terms the average young player can easily follow. Too much written tennis instruction is overly detailed and unnecessarily complicated for young readers. This book allows intermediate readers to learn the basic strokes of the game using easy-to-follow instructions. But what really makes this instructional guidebook fun is the blend of instruction with Manga characters. Manga is a Japanese art form loved by children and young adults all over the world. And truly, with the accompaniment of characters, each lesson not only piques the reader's interest in learning the strokes themselves, but it also promotes their reading skills and drives them to understand what they are reading—the instruction relative to a game they wish to learn.

Additionally, during the many months that I worked on this project, I came to the inescapable conclusion that the young readers of this book will want to make their own simplifications of the game and personalize their own approaches to improvement. In a nutshell, young players will begin to take responsibility for their own games—and that is a good thing.

And finally, young people: As you read and apply the tips I have provided, I hope you realize that this book is not meant to replace the teaching of your local certified professional. It is extremely difficult for you to teach yourself tennis. There is simply too much to learn about the game. In fact, your teaching pro may disagree with some of the ideas presented here, but don't worry, because there is no one way to play the game. You may experience some difficulties in executing the strokes properly at first, but you must allow yourself some time to gain confidence in your new strokes. You may even drop a match or two as you learn new techniques. But if you are not willing to experiment, you will not improve. Above all, the one thing I hope you will learn is that improvement only comes with hard work and patience, as I know all too well.

Steven White, instructor
Professional Tennis Registry

how do i hold the racquet?

When an inexperienced player takes his or her first tennis lesson, the first question that student might ask is, "How do I hold the racquet?" To answer that question, I would normally say, "Use any of the four basic grips that are used in the game of tennis." I might also say, "Use any grip that is comfortable to you." And for the beginning child, that is exactly what I recommend. But for all practical purposes, I'm going to try to teach you each of the four grips used in today's game. Then, as you improve, you can experiment with each of them until you find the one that works best for you.

How a player grips the racquet has a lot to do with how that player plays the game. Each grip has specific uses to apply spins and produce power. Traditionally, the grips are called the eastern, western, continental, and two-handed grips. Each grip has its benefits and limitations. For example, the continental grip can be used to hit almost every shot in tennis, but with limited power and spin. The western grip is used to impart heavy topspin on the ball, but players using this grip tend to have trouble with low bouncing balls, and miss-hits are a common occurrence due to the extreme angle of the swing pattern. Players new to the game should begin play using the eastern forehand and backhand grips because the face of the racquet is naturally square with the ball at impact when using a relatively level swing pattern.

1

how to check your grip size

Before learning the different types of grips, take a moment to check that your racquet's handle is the right size for you. There are many different ways to determine grip size, but the one I prefer is shown in the drawing below. Hold the racquet normally with your fingers spread a little. Then check to see that your thumb and middle finger overlap from the first knuckle to the tips. If your grip feels too small, it probably is. You should use the largest grip size possible because that will help you feel the ball better, give you more control, and reduce the risk of arm or wrist injury.

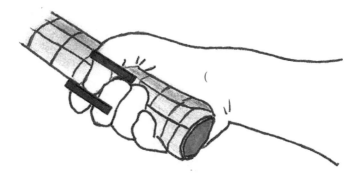

2 eastern (shake hands) grip

The grip most often taught by instructors and teachers is the eastern grip. To get to the eastern forehand grip, sometimes called the "shake hands grip," start with the palm of your hand on the strings and let your hand slide down the throat and handle of the racquet, then grip and "shake hands" with the racquet. Another way to get to the grip is to place the "V" created between the index finger and thumb of your racquet hand on the upper beveled edge of the racquet handle to hit a forehand. For righties, use the upper right beveled edge; for lefties, use the upper left beveled edge.

3 eastern backhand grip

You must switch your grip from forehand to backhand to use the eastern grips appropriately. If you use the forehand grip to hit a backhand ground stroke, your racquet face will be tilted back too much at impact and the ball will pop up in the air. You must change your grip to hit a backhand.

To get to the eastern backhand grip, simply rotate your hand to the left until the "V" is lined up with the upper left beveled edge of the racquet handle (for left-handed players, the upper right beveled edge). The effect is that the racquet face is more nearly vertical as you hit the ball. One of the benefits of using the eastern grips for your ground strokes is that you can use a variety of spins on your shots.

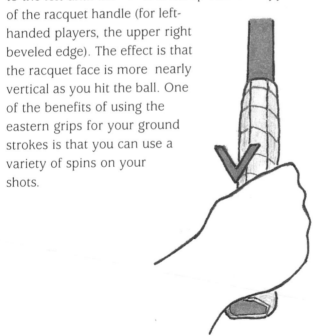

4 western grip

The more extreme of the grips is the western grip. It is generally used by more advanced players who want to hit high looping shots with excessive topspin. With this grip, the racquet hand is even further behind the handle than with the eastern grip.

Place the "V" created between the index finger and thumb on the right or left beveled edge of the racquet handle, depending on the player's dominant hand—about three o'clock for a right-hander's forehand and about nine o'clock for a lefties' forehand. To hit backhands, it would be the opposite. I do not recommend the western grip to beginners or intermediate players because it is difficult to meet the ball squarely at impact. The swing pattern is too extreme. To execute consistent ground strokes using this grip, a player must possess a strong wrist and excellent timing.

5 the continental (all-purpose) grip

The continental grip, sometimes called the "all purpose grip," can be used in the execution of any basic shot in tennis, including the serve, volley, overhead smash, and all ground strokes. Although this grip is versatile, it is lacking in the ability to produce increased power and topspin on ground strokes. The continental grip can be effectively used to impart underspin on ground strokes, and to hit volleys without changing your grip. This is an excellent grip for some beginners because you don't have to change your grip during the playing of a point. As your skills improve, you can try other grips, which will allow you to hit more spins with more power, accuracy, and control.

6 the two-handed grip

The two-handed grip is generally used for the backhand side only. Although you can use two hands off both sides if you choose to, I don't recommend it because it's difficult to switch grips from forehand to backhand. The two-handed grip is formed by placing your racquet hand on the bottom of the handle and your free hand above it. The free hand should be in an eastern forehand position, while the racquet hand can be in any position that is comfortable to you. I recommend a continental position for the racquet hand.

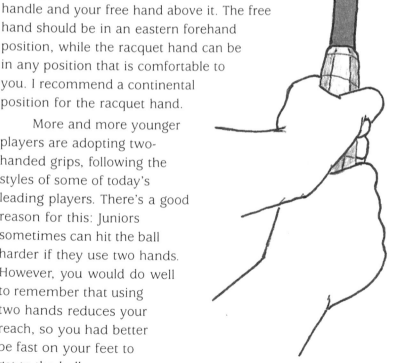

More and more younger players are adopting two-handed grips, following the styles of some of today's leading players. There's a good reason for this: Juniors sometimes can hit the ball harder if they use two hands. However, you would do well to remember that using two hands reduces your reach, so you had better be fast on your feet to get to the ball.

how to hit a better forehand

For most players, new or experienced, the forehand is the shot on which you can count, when the rest of your game falls apart. A stroke to call on at critical times during the course of a match, the forehand is the big weapon.

Most players learn the forehand first because it's a familiar motion to them. Since childhood, the acts of throwing a ball, swinging a baseball bat, or rolling a bowling ball are all similar motions that relate to the forehand in some way or another. The instrument or object is taken back behind you in a backswing fashion and released or thrown by stepping in or leaning in with your body.

At any rate, I recommend to all beginners to learn the forehand first. It is important to learn the stroke properly from the start and to avoid slipping into bad habits as your game develops.

1 be ready to move

How you stand when you are waiting for your opponent to hit the ball has an enormous impact on your shot-making abilities and effectiveness.

Standing with your racquet out in front of your body, leaning slightly forward, knees flexed, and your body weight evenly distributed on the balls of your feet, is called a ready stance. Assuming you already have established good court position, it is important to get into a ready stance when waiting for your opponent to hit the ball back to your side of the net. The ready stance keeps you poised to move in any direction and ready to react to any shot your opponent might hit.

If, like many juniors, you are better on the forehand side, you should wait with a forehand grip and make a quick grip change if the ball comes to the backhand side.

2 prepare on the run

If the ball is relatively close to you on your forehand side, it's a fairly simple matter to get sideways and skip into position with your racquet back. But on a wide forehand, you actually have to run to the ball. You may have little time to position yourself and hit smoothly. To make the best shot possible, take big running strides to get close to the ball, then smaller, rapid, stutter steps to get into final position. Your racquet should be going back as you run, and your last step should be toward the oncoming ball with your forward foot. If possible, you should not be running as you hit the ball because your body weight will be moving sideways, and you will keep on going after you have made contact. So try to get to the ball with time to spare, enough for you to pause before you begin swinging. Doing this will enable you to recover and get back into good position for your next shot.

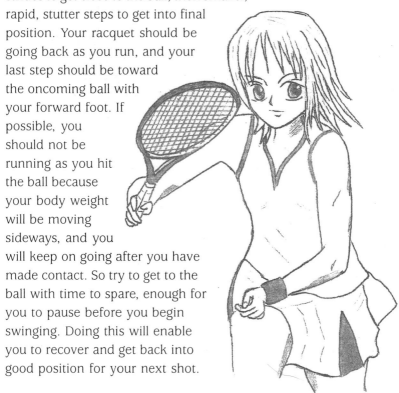

3 turn your shoulders and get your racquet all the way back

On ground strokes, the most common mistake among young players is not getting their racquets back and ready quickly enough. As soon as you realize that you are about to hit a forehand, position yourself sideways and start your racquet head moving back. Turn your upper body first so that your racquet head, your arm and shoulder move as one unit. Then keep your racquet head moving for a full backswing.

At the end of your backswing, your racquet should be at least slightly above your waist to insure a full backswing. Occasionally, freeze your racquet during practice to make sure you are getting it back as far as you should. A full backswing permits you to make a strong swing at the ball— not a halfhearted one. Additionally, you should keep your weight slightly forward, ready for the swing toward the ball. At the completion of the backswing, pivot on your rear foot so you can push off and transfer your weight forward into the shot.

4 concentrate on the hitting zone

The hitting zone is the area where the racquet makes contact with the ball. As it should be, this zone is one of the most critical parts of your forehand swing. For most junior players, the hitting zone starts in front of the rear hip and continues to the point where the racquet is almost level with the front foot. Your objective should be to keep the ball on the strings for as much of that area as possible (highlighted between the racquets). The teaching pros say you can do this by hitting smoothly through the ball. The longer you can do that, the more control you will have over your shot. You should really concentrate on the ball in that hitting zone.

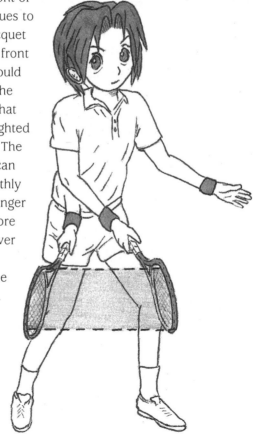

Do your best to actually see the ball making contact with the strings—definitely a challenging process physically.

5 finish the shot and your follow-through

From the hitting zone, move the racquet into a full follow-through to complete the shot.

Let your arm swing around your body until the racquet is up by your shoulder. As your follow-through comes to an end, try not to let the palm of your hand turn up. It is better to allow your hand to come around with the palm facing down a little rather than up. If you turn your palm up, the ball will fly up too high.

Try not to use too much wrist as you make your shot. If you roll your wrist in an attempt to put excessive spin on the ball, you will probably hit a weak and erratic shot.

I also like to exhale as I follow through because it helps me concentrate. You might like to try that too. Simply exhale sharply the way karate students are taught to do when they learn to punch or chop.

learning to hit backhands

In today's power game, many of the top pros have better backhands than forehands. That's largely because the backhand is a more natural stroke since the arms open up across your body instead of closing around it as they do on the forehand. And in almost all cases, those who hit the backhand well have developed the stroke by putting more time and effort into it.

Roger Federer is one of the smoothest ball-strikers on the pro tour. He is equally effective off both sides, and he is a dangerous opponent, no matter which ground stroke he hits. Like Roger, if you wish to be strong off both sides from the baseline, you must practice, practice, practice.

1 turn your shoulders first

For the early backswing that is so essential to a good backhand you must do two things:

First, you have to sharpen your sense of anticipation so you can make the quick decision to take your opponent's ball on the backhand side. Secondly, you should turn your shoulders as soon as you make your choice. A rapid shoulder turn will get you sideways to the ball and will automatically start your racquet moving back for that early backswing. Of course, you may also have to move into position to make your shot. If that is the case, turn your shoulders as you move. By the time you arrive at the point where you are going to hit the ball, your racquet should be fully back.

2 get your racquet all the way back

Draw your racquet back as far as you can. Don't pull it part of the way back, pause, then swing forward. That kind of halfway stroke will produce a halfhearted shot. For power and consistency, take a full swing at the ball—using one smooth motion from backswing to the forward swing to the follow-through.

Notice that the racquet head is relatively high at the end of the backswing because this player has a looping action on his backhand. Other players may prefer a straight backswing which puts the racquet about waist-high at the completion of the backswing.

How you take your racquet back is much less important than getting the racquet all the way back and bringing it forward so that the head is rising slightly through the hitting zone.

3 step out to meet the ball

The best way to hit a powerful backhand is *not* accomplished by swinging as hard as you can. As with any ground stroke, the most effective way to hit shots with force behind them is by stepping into your shot. If you step out to meet the ball just before impact, you will transfer weight into your shot, giving you the power you need. When you complete your hit, all of your weight should be on your front foot. But remember, it is important to remain balanced at the end of the stroke, so keep the toes of your back foot on the ground.

4 bring your racquet up to meet the ball

Since most backhand ground strokes are made close to the baseline, the ball will have to travel nearly the full length of the court to get the depth you should have on your shot. That is not hard to do—provided you hit the ball high enough over the net. A net-skimmer will have to be hit exceptionally hard to go deep into your opponent's court. You should hit the ball so that you lift it several feet over the net. You can do this more easily if you bring your racquet forward on a gently rising plane to meet the ball and swing from low to high.

5 keep the ball on the strings

Make contact with the ball just in front of your forward foot and keep the ball on the strings as long as possible. The racquet face should travel on a straight upward line through the hitting zone in the direction you want the ball to go. If you are trying to hit the ball crosscourt, make contact a little farther out in front. If you are trying to send the ball down the line, make contact a little later, closer to your forward foot. In either case, you will increase your accuracy if you keep the ball on the strings for as long as you can. So, at impact, do not swing your racquet around quickly.

Instead, push it out in front along the line that you want the ball to go. As you hit through the ball, your weight should be moving forward to add extra power to the shot.

6 meet the ball squarely and firmly

Many juniors seem to have a fear of using backhand strokes. And when they do hit a backhand stroke, they try to get rid of the ball as quickly as possible. Instead of hitting through the ball, they slap at it. Often, the problem is that the player opens up to the court too quickly, leading with the wrist or elbow. Thus, he or she has to swing the racquet in a fishtailing motion, which is a recipe for disaster. When you hit a backhand, your racquet, wrist, and forearm should move as one unit until the ball leaves your racquet. If you are hitting a two-handed backhand, allow your hips and shoulders to help you guide the racquet head through the ball.

7 hitting the one-handed slice

Most players that use a one-handed backhand usually have some variety in their shots off that side. Usually, this includes a slice backhand. The slice backhand is probably one of the most natural strokes in tennis. Bringing your racquet back to about shoulder height position on the backswing is as natural as blinking your eyes. The trick is in knowing what to do with the racquet from shoulder height position. Most beginners wind up chopping down at the ball, missing it completely, or they impart too much spin on the ball which causes it to float or pop up in the air with little or no pace.

The slice backhand is accomplished by having your racquet head tilted at impact instead of swinging at the ball with a severely angled swing pattern. It needs less effort than a topspin shot, and the ball's pace and depth can be controlled. The motion involved in slicing your backhand is the reverse of the natural topspin forehand. Take your racquet back shoulder high, come down to meet the ball, and follow through in front of you. If your racquet head is moving down as you hit the ball, you will brush the back of it and that will put underspin on it. The slice backhand may be used for deep penetrating shots or to create angles to move your opponent around the court. The slice backhand can also be used to attack the net. The underspin created by slicing the ball keeps the ball low on its bounce, making it a little more difficult for your opponent to hit a passing shot.

8 keep your racquet up

As you complete your backhand, you should follow through as far out in front as possible. A full follow-through will insure that you hit through the ball and do not slow the racquet head down before the ball leaves the strings. It will also help you complete your weight transfer so that you finish with virtually all of your weight on your front foot. To make sure you are following through completely, freeze your position at the end of the stroke during one of your practice sessions. Your racquet head should be as high as your head and point out toward the target area. As your backhand improves, you can extend your follow-through to generate even more power on your shot.

A proper follow-through will not only give you more control over your shot, but it will actually force you to open up your body to the court as you complete your stroke, facilitating the recovery process as you prepare for your next shot.

are two hands better than one?

Everywhere people play tennis, from the public parks to professional stadiums and arenas, you see people of all ages using two hands on the backhand side. The two-handed backhand boom is here to stay. Back in the 1940s, players like Pancho Segura came onto the scene using two hands in a professional atmosphere for the first time. Since then, we have seen a significant number of pros rise to the top using two hands on the backhand side—Chris Evert, Jimmy Connors, Bjorn Borg, Andre Agassi, Maria Sharapova, Raphael Nadal, and the list goes on.

Today's teaching pros are following suit. I would be willing to bet that ninety percent of today's youngsters start out hitting two-handed backhands. I started out using two hands on the backhand side because I needed the other hand on the racquet for more power and control. Although I switched to a one-handed backhand, as I got older and stronger, many two-handed players continue to use the two-handed backhand throughout their careers.

Yes, the two-handed backhand can be a powerful weapon, but it has limitations. Sometimes your reach is limited, and in other times it is difficult to get out of the way of a ball coming right you. If you like the two-handed shot, at least adapt a one-handed shot to get extra reach on wide hit balls. One great plus for the two-handed backhand is that you can learn to disguise the direction of your shots with a flick of the wrists. Racquet technology and the overall improvement of athletic conditioning has made this possible, raising the level of all shot-making in tennis and contributing to the effectiveness of the two-handed shot.

when two hands help

I want to emphasize from the start that two-handed strokes are not for everyone. If you can hit effective one-handed ground strokes, then you should work on improving them rather than attempting to switch to a two-handed stroke. If you have a weak grip, however, two hands will give you the extra strength you need to hit a powerful shot. A youngster will often have trouble gripping the racquet with one hand on the backhand side because the hand is pulling the racquet rather than pushing it forward. Thus, the extra hand can go behind the handle for extra support.

2 how to hit with topspin

It seems that every young kid wants to hit a two-handed backhand with topspin like Raphael Nadal or Andy Roddick. That is not so unusual, I suppose, since many kids tried to serve and volley like Pete Sampras when he was the world's leading player. But, face it, most youngsters do not possess the extraordinary skills of a Nadal or Roddick. Nadal's uncanny shot is the result of enormous strength in his wrists and arms, coupled with precise timing. If that timing if off even just a little, his game can go to pieces. So I do not suggest that you try to hit the Nadal way. However, you can learn to put topspin on the ball using a two-handed backhand simply by looping your backswing and hitting the ball with the racquet, moving from low to high at contact. The more the racquet is moving upward, the more topspin you will put on the ball. Do not try to roll the racquet head over the ball at impact— that will do nothing for your spin, and you will probably hit the ball straight into the net or the ground. Keep the head vertical as the player in this drawing is doing.

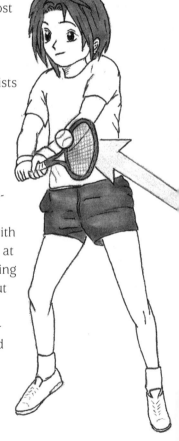

44 • bring your racquet

3 use one hand for extra reach

Two-handed shots reduce your ability to get to wide balls because the trailing arm limits your reach. For example, there is no way the player in this picture could get her racquet on the ball if she used a two-handed backhand. You have to be closer to the ball when you use two hands than you do with one in order to hit an effective shot. That means you have to be fast on your feet so you can get into position quickly or be prepared to use one hand occasionally for very wide balls like this player is doing. The pros say that you have to be one-half step faster to hit a wide shot with two hands. That may not sound like a lot, but it can make the difference between hitting the ball or missing it.

learning to volley

To volley means to hit the ball before it bounces while standing near or at the net. Naturally, you do not start out the point at the net unless you are playing doubles. If you are playing singles, you have to make a transition from the baseline to get to the net, which is accomplished in several different situations.

For example, during the course of a rally from the baseline, your opponent may hit a drop shot which brings you to the net, or you may have an aggressive game where you attack the net. In either case, you are at the net. What do you do now?

First of all, do not panic and try to recover back to the baseline. You will get caught in the middle of your side of the court, called "no-mans land"—a vulnerable court position. Stand your ground and prepare to volley.

You should use a grip that will work off both sides. You do not have a lot of time to prepare since you are closer to your opponent, so changing your grip from forehand to backhand could be a handicap. I recommend the use of a continental grip. With this grip, you can hit off both sides without changing.

Beginners would not be wrong to use the grips used for ground strokes. As you improve, you can experiment with a grip you do not have to change at the net.

Your second concern should be reminding yourself *not* to take a full backswing as you prepare to hit a volley. Taking a full backswing could cause you to be late making contact with the ball. The volley is a short, quick stroke that should be executed almost instinctively.

Net play is usually fast-paced, so your next concern should be to keep it simple. Many junior players have poor volleys because they believe it is a shot that you do not have to practice since you are so close to the net. On the contrary, not practicing your volleys can be disastrous. Missing the easy put-away also can be an embarrassing situation, so practice your volleys and keep it short and simple.

1 wait with your racquet up

You should keep your racquet head high when you are playing at the net. The tip of your racquet head should be just below eye level so you can move the racquet quickly to either side as you move to make contact with the ball. It is important to keep your racquet up because most of the balls you have to volley will be at the net or higher.

2 keep your weight forward

Keep your weight forward, on the balls of your feet, so you can step out quickly to reach wide balls. Your eyes should be glued to the ball as your opponent hits it. Also, it is a good idea to use your other hand to steady, support, and guide the racquet as you prepare to volley.

3 turn the racquet, turn your shoulders

Because time is so short at the net, you should use little or no backswing when hitting a volley. In fact, I hesitate to say the word "backswing" in connection with the volley, because I prefer that beginners use virtually no backswing at all on the shot. From the ready position, turn your racquet so that the strings face the ball.

Then, simply meet the ball out in front of you. As your volleying improves, you can take a short backswing by turning your shoulders and opening the face of the racquet with the racquet still held high. You should not let the racquet go further back than your shoulder. If you find that you are miss-timing or miss-hitting the ball, shorten your swing again until you are meeting the ball squarely.

4 step out to meet the ball

Whether you are hitting a forehand or a backhand, whenever you have enough time, you should move toward the ball as you hit your volleys.

Being in the right place is half the battle when you are volleying. If you can get to the ball, then you can hit it. Take short, rapid steps to get to the ball, and make your final step with the foot farthest from the ball. The last step will allow you to stretch out for the ball if you have misjudged its flight. You will also be moving your weight into your shot, which will give you a little extra power.

More importantly, you will be properly balanced and ready to recover for your next shot.

5 the backhand volley

The backhand volley is one of the easiest tennis shots to hit—provided that you keep things simple. There is almost nothing to the shot, because the backswing is very short and the forward swing is just a swift, punching motion without a long follow-through. The problem, of course, is that you have very little time at the net to get into position to make a precise and well-controlled shot. The ball is coming at you so fast that you have to hit it instinctively. That means your volleys should be grooved through lots of practice, so you never have to think about them during your matches.

If your volley goes sour when you play, simplify it—cut down on your backswing and shorten your forward swing. Most volleying errors made by young, inexperienced players are caused by trying to do too much with a stroke that should be kept simple.

6 defend with the backhand volley

Sometimes, when you are at the net, a ball blasted directly at you can be hard to handle. How do you deal with it? You will rarely have time to get out of the way and hit a normal volley.

The best response is to use your backhand volley to defend yourself and to get the ball back. Your backhand volley can cover most of your upper body, while you would have to move out of the way of the ball to hit a decent forehand volley. Using the backhand, you can still hit a respectable volley since you have the room to make a short punching stroke. On occasion, though, it is enough simply to hold the racquet firmly and block the ball back, using the pace that is already on it. As with any shot, your main concern should be to get the ball back over the net.

To practice this stroke, have your hitting partner direct shots into your body. As you get more comfortable, your partner should move closer and gradually hit the ball harder.

developing a reliable serve

When you mess up a ground stroke or volley, it may be because your opponent hit you a difficult ball. But when you mess up your serve, there is only one person at fault—and that person is you. The serve is the one shot where you are completely in control, where you have no one to blame but yourself if you do not hit it right. To serve well, you must begin by learning to toss the ball properly. In fact, the ball toss is the cornerstone of a consistent and reliable serve. If you toss the ball in the right spot every time, you will be rewarded with a solid delivery. On the other hand, if you consistently toss the ball too far out or behind you, you will have to settle for a high number of embarrassing double faults. So let's examine the way to develop the dependable toss you need for a reliable serve.

1

get comfortable

To achieve a consistent toss, first get yourself comfortable. Step up to the baseline, take a deep breath, and then breath normally. Do not rush your serve—there is no hurry, and your opponent is not going anywhere.

Your front foot should be at a slight angle to the baseline, putting your upper body at roughly the same angle. Adjust your position until you feel comfortable. At this point, feel free to bounce the ball a couple of times—it can help.

When you are ready, start your motion with your racquet in front of you, cradled by the hand that is holding the ball. Your hands should always start from the same position to facilitate the rhythm of the motion.

2 a grip for beginners

If you are a beginner learning to serve, you perhaps should start using a forehand grip. In the serving ready position, the strings will be facing almost straight down. As you swing the racquet down and around, the strings will meet the ball straight on, and you will have a better chance of hitting the serve in the proper area of the court.

But your serve will be limited to a spinless, pushing motion if you do not change to a continental grip. Use the forehand grip only until you develop some basic feel and control of the racquet during the serve. Then switch to the continental grip. Doing this will give you added power and control on your serve.

3 open your arms

I like to think of the serve as a three-part action: tossing the ball, raising the racquet, and swinging at the ball. However, the first two should be done simultaneously—you should toss the ball and raise your racquet at the same time.

To do this, open your arms. From the ready position, your arms should drop together and then come up as though you were forming separate halves of a large circle.

Bring both of your arms up at the same speed, and you will not have any problems timing your serve. Make sure your arms go all the way down before they start up again.

Practice this motion with a ball and racquet for a while before releasing the ball in the air. Repeat it until you develop a smooth action. Then practice letting go of the ball.

4 reach up to let go of the ball

Although we call the action a "toss," you should not throw the ball into the air. The idea is to reach. The momentum from this motion should be sufficient to take the ball high enough in the air for you to swing your racquet and make proper contact.

If you are moving into your serve, your body will also be moving up to give you a little extra reach as you release the ball. If you "throw" the ball from around shoulder height or below, as many beginning players tend to do, your toss will be erratic, resulting in an inconsistent serve.

5 toss the ball to your highest reach

I see many junior players who toss the ball too high or too low. The ball should only travel as high as you can reach with your racquet.

If you toss it higher than that, the ball will be falling, giving you a harder target to hit. If you toss the ball too low, you will have a cramped swing which will have little power and even less control.

The ball should travel only about three feet, a little in front and a little to the right (if you are right-handed) to complete a smooth and rhythmic serve.

6 snap your wrist and follow through

If you snap your wrist and hit your serve with a throwing motion, you will move the racquet head faster through contact. Most tennis strokes, of course, should be hit with a firm wrist, but the serve needs that wrist motion to add extra power to the stroke. At contact you should snap your wrist forward and then continue the snap into the follow-through. You do not need brute force for a powerful serve—it is more a matter of putting the pieces together at the right time, and the wrist snap is one of the most important components.

But the serve does not stop with the wrist snap and contact. Let the racquet head flow into the follow-through in an arc which is as big as possible. If you stop your follow-through prematurely, your racquet head will be slowing down as you hit the ball. That means you will not be getting maximum power, and you will be wasting much of the effort that you put into your backswing. Hurl yourself into the serve with a big sweep of your racquet into the follow-through. Your racquet arm should swing across your body so that the racquet head ends up on the opposite side of your body.

Check yourself occasionally in practice by stopping after you have served and note the position of your racquet head. If it is behind you, your follow-through was good.

using the lob

The lob is one of the most underestimated and under used shots in tennis. Few players, even at experienced levels, appreciate its full effectiveness. They seldom practice it and, as a result, they are reluctant to use it during competitive play. That is a shame because the lob can be a valuable tool in many different situations in a match, and it is not a tough shot to hit.

Here are a few of the situations where the lob may be effective during the course of a match.

1

when you are out of position

For the average player, the most important time to use the lob is when you are pulled out of position and you need a shot that will give you time to recover and get back into the point. For example, if a player hits a shot sharply with a lot of angle that pulls you completely off the court, you can make the best of the situation by returning the shot with a lob that is high and deep. The height will give you time to hustle back to the center of the baseline, and the depth will keep your opponent back on the baseline.

So when you are out of position, hit a lob that is high and deep—and preferably crosscourt to give yourself more court to work with.

2 discouraging the net rusher

Another excellent time to use a lob is when you are facing an opponent who constantly charges the net— particularly if you find it hard to pass with shots to the side. Send up a lob that will clear the top of your opponent's outstretched racquet and drop it behind the other player.

The lob should go deep, but it will not necessarily need the height required when you are just trying to stay in the point. And who knows—if you surprise your opponent, your shot may even be a winner!

3 tiring out your opponent

Hitting a lot of overheads can wear a player down. So, if you figure that you are in for a long, closely-fought match, you can tire your opponent by sending up lob after lob, forcing the other player to chase down the ball and hit overheads. Even if your opponent recognizes your ploy and returns your lobs with ground strokes, it will still be wearying. A ball that drops as steeply as a lob has no pace or forward momentum on it and has to be hit hard for an effective return. So you can use your lob to tire your opponent even when he or she is playing most of the points from the baseline.

4 disguise

Keep in mind that most players never expect a lob out of the blue. Also keep in mind that a lob is basically a ground stroke and can be easily disguised. So, prepare as you would a ground stroke and hit your lobs the length of the court and high enough in the air to be effective.

To disguise your lob, take a full backswing. In fact, take the racquet back with the same motion that you would use for a normal forehand or backhand ground stroke, so your opponent cannot tell what kind shot you are going to hit until you contact the ball.

If you have enough time, turn sideways to the ball, take your racquet all the way back, and step toward the ball as you begin your forward swing. Meet the ball with a slightly tilted racquet head to lift the ball over your opponent's head.

the overhead smash

The overhead smash is not an easy shot. It takes coordination, timing, and practice to master. But it is worth the effort because, done right, it will often be a winner. The reason many young players have trouble with the overhead is that they whale away at the ball, trying to blast it past an opponent—which is why they suffer the embarrassment of a complete miss or a wild miss-hit. Instead, like the serve, the overhead should be a controlled shot, hit carefully and placed properly. In fact, if you can serve adequately, you can develop a reliable overhead.

Most of your overhead opportunities will come when you are playing at the net and your opponent sends up a lob attempting to send you into the backcourt. You will not know until your opponent has hit the ball whether you are going to have to hit a volley or move back for a smash, so you should be prepared for either.

1 get sideways

When you realize that you are going to have to hit an overhead, your very first movement should be to raise your racquet hand up to shoulder level and turn sideways to the flight of the ball. That shoulder turn will get your racquet moving back and let you bring your other hand up to start tracking the ball.

If the lob is short, that may be all that you will have time to do before swinging at the ball. The chances are, however, that you will have to move back to get into the right position to meet the ball.

2 shuffle back

Good footwork is essential on the overhead. As you are preparing your racquet for the shot, you will probably have to retreat a few steps deeper into your court. Use short, sideways skipping steps. Shuffling back permits you to move backward, yet still keep your center of gravity forward. Stay on your toes. You sometimes see young players fall down on overheads; they lose their balance because they are moving backward with their weight on their heels. If you skip back on your toes, it will help you remain balanced.

3 keep the ball in front of you

It is not always easy to determine how far a lob is going to sail into your court. Many young players get into trouble because they let the ball descend behind them. When that happens, it is difficult to hit any kind of decent shot. Always be sure the ball remains in front of you as you retreat from the net. If you happen to back up too far, it is simple enough to step forward again to meet the ball.

Stay behind the ball whether you are taking it on the fly or after the ball has bounced.

4 make contact out in front and follow through

When you bring your racquet up to meet the ball, you should hit it in front of your body. Your body should also be fully extended upward and a little forward at impact. That way, you will be sure that your weight is moving properly forward as you meet the ball. You should be transferring your weight forward by pushing off your back foot, but remember to keep that foot on the ground so that you stay balanced.

After you have hit the ball, keep the racquet moving down and across your body to ensure a good follow-through. Doing this will complete your swing and give you more control on your shot.

returning serve

If the serve is the most important shot in tennis, getting it back should be your next priority. The service return is not just another ground stroke. Matches are won and lost with service returns. If your opponent has a booming serve, you are most vulnerable. Developing a consistent service return is crucial.

The first step in developing a consistent return is to get organized. Before you step up to the line to return serve, walk around the baseline area to get your thoughts together. Consider the score, choose a grip, take notice of where your opponent has been serving—do anything to develop a consistent routine. It also helps to have in mind a specific area of the court you would like to hit. This will help you relax and improve your shot-making.

Then, get your racquet moving. The ball is going to be on top of you quickly, so get your racquet to the appropriate side. Turn your shoulders, but take a shorter backswing if your opponent has a fast serve. Most young and inexperienced players make the mistake of taking a big backswing, causing them to be late making contact with the ball. Try to develop a chip shot when returning against big servers. The chip is like hitting a volley, except off the bounce.

Finally, stay down when returning serve. There should be no wasted motion. Bend your knees and stay on the same horizontal plane as the approaching ball and your forward swing. Get your eyes near the level of the ball, and focus on the point of contact.

hitting an approach shot

An approach shot is any shot hit from inside the baseline in an attempt to get to the net and make an offensive stand. The first and most important factor in hitting a well-executed approach shot is in choosing the appropriate ball to come in on. In order to attack the net safely, you should wait until your opponent hits a shot that lands well inside the baseline. If you try to attack and hit an approach shot from too deep in the court, you might be giving your opponent an opportunity to pass you at the net.

For beginners and intermediate players, I recommend that you wait until your opponent's shot lands inside the service line before you attempt an approach shot. When hitting an approach shot, your target area should be deep into your opponent's court, near the baseline.

down the line or cross-court

It is a good idea to hit your approach shots down the line, instead of cross-court, for a couple of reasons. The first reason is that the angle of your opponent's passing shot is reduced. The second reason is that the ball spends less time in the air, giving your opponent less time to react.

However, there may be a situation when you might *not* want to hit your approach shots down the line. For example, your opponent could be out of position, giving you an open court to hit into with a cross-court approach.

In either case, the fundamentals of hitting an approach shot are basically like those of a ground stroke, but you must take a shorter backswing. Remember you are closer to the net than you would be during a baseline rally, so you do not need to hit a full ground stroke to have an effective approach. Lower the risk of over-hitting by making a more controllable swing and by taking a shorter backswing. The name of the game on the approach shot is to control the ball so you can place it accurately.

2 keep moving after you have hit the shot

Like all shots in tennis, focus on the point of contact. In this case, you will want to make sure that you are making contact well out in front and staying with your shot for pinpoint accuracy. It is important that you do not rush yourself when making an approach shot. Once you see that your opponent has hit a ball landing short on your side off the net and you have made the decision to come to the net, move forward immediately and take your racquet back. Take your time in producing the stroke.

Since you have made a commitment to come in, keep moving after you have hit the shot.

When watching the pros, you will notice that they run through their approach shots. This is an acquired skill. Hitting on the move requires excellent timing and can be learned with practice.

using the drop shot

The drop shot is a relatively soft shot that travels with a low trajectory barely clearing the net and lands very short on your opponent's side of the net. Many young and inexperienced players make the mistake of thinking that the drop shot should be an outright winner. Realistically speaking, the drop shot should be thought of as a setup stroke. It is designed to draw a weak reply from your opponent, putting him or her in a vulnerable situation.

The drop shot should bounce low, forcing your opponent to hit up on the ball while drawing him or her closer to the net. A high bouncing dropper will give your opponent an opportunity to drive down on the ball resulting in a winner.

I recommend that the drop shot be hit with underspin—the more, the better. Putting underspin on your drop shot will cause the ball to bite the court a little and stop the forward momentum of the flight of the ball. But be careful: Attempting to apply too much underspin can cause your shot to pop up, giving your opponent plenty of time to run down your drop shot, putting you in a vulnerable position.

1 choosing the right time

Choosing the right time to attempt a drop shot is crucial. You should only try hitting the drop shot from inside the baseline. All too often, I see young players attempting drop shots from behind the baseline. This is difficult to accomplish for two reasons. First, you are too far away from the net, making it a difficult shot to execute. Second, the ball has to travel too far, giving your opponent time to read the shot and enabling him or her to effectively retrieve your shot. The best time to attempt a drop shot is when you are inside the baseline and your opponent is behind the baseline.

The drop shot is another one of those shots that players neglect to practice. To practice drop shots, start out hitting them from about the service line. As you develop some confidence, you can move further back and bounce the ball shorter in your opponent's court.

executing the half-volley

What is a half-volley? It is not a volley, nor is it a full-fledged ground stroke, even though it is hit off the bounce. Usually, the half-volley is used when the ball bounces almost at your feet. Imagine yourself in transition, trying to get to the net from the baseline. You have just hit an approach shot, and you are closing in to get to the net. Suddenly your opponent hits a shot that just clears the net and you aren't close enough to hit a volley before it bounces, and you aren't back far enough to hit a ground stroke. What do you do? Since the ball is literally at your feet, you have to get the racquet down to the level of the ball.

1 bend your knees

Bend your knees and upper body to get the racquet head low enough to make solid contact. If you simply drop the racquet head down to make contact, it will be difficult to control the shot. Bend down far enough to get your racquet hand and the racquet itself on the same horizontal plane. There is virtually no backswing with the half-volley. Get down, take the racquet to either the forehand or backhand side, keep the racquet in a parallel position to the court, and simply block the ball with a firm grip and wrist.

For a solid half-volley, try to make contact with the ball immediately after the bounce and use a short follow-through in the direction you want the ball to go.

2 follow through and keep moving

The follow-through for the half-volley is very much like that of a conventional volley. The half-volley is not a powerful stroke, so there is no need for a long, sweeping follow-through. Keep it short so you can recover quickly and be on your way to the net without a pause in your forward movement. Although the half-volley is often a defensive shot you are forced to use because you have not had enough time to get close enough to hit a real volley, do not let that keep you from taking the offensive. After the half-volley, you should continue up toward the net so that your next shot can be a conventional volley. If you have hit a good half-volley, your body momentum will be moving forward after you have hit the ball.

Even the fastest players can be under pressure when forced to hit the half-volley. When you are under pressure to hit a half-volley, concentrate on getting your hand down by bending your knees and keeping your racquet head up. Be sure to grip the racquet tightly and keep a firm wrist to hit the ball firmly. The sooner you can take the ball off the bounce, the better your half-volley will be.

the secret weapon

using your head to win

Tennis is not just a game that requires physical prowess – it has mental demands as well. It is difficult to pinpoint exactly what percentage is physical and what percentage is mental, but as the level of play rises, mental concentration is even more important.

Experienced players use their minds on court. They get to the next level of play by concentrating and focusing their minds on the task of winning every point, one at a time. They open their minds to strategic and tactical thinking to avoid playing the game mindlessly. And they instill confidence and belief in themselves by choosing to think positively about their games, regardless of the score.

1 concentrate on every hit

Players who win many more matches than they lose advance their games by learning to concentrate on every hit, no matter who is on the other side of the net. They have discovered that to perform well consistently requires the ability to concentrate consistently. To play well against all levels of players is no easy task. In fact, it is often easier to play well and concentrate better against tougher opponents since minds wander out of boredom or lack of intensity against lesser opponents.

Whether it is match play or practice, improving your concentration should be your goal every time you take to the courts. By consistently concentrating well on the court you will develop your mind much like you work to develop your strokes. You will be able to bring your best play to the courts on a regular basis, no matter who your opponent is. Notice the calm intensity on the face of the player in this illustration.

As your mind develops over time, the bottom line is that you will become a better thinker on the court. You will probably become better at spotting weaknesses across the net the longer you play the game and the more experience you acquire. Learn to analyze your own game as well as your opponent's each time you play. Tailor your strategies to suit your style of play and the game needed against your opponent. Remember to think positively. What is the use of using your head to win if you are brainwashing yourself for defeat?

2 maintain a winning attitude

Nothing can hurt your game more than a negative attitude and a lack of enthusiasm. Ask yourself a question: Who is responsible for your attitude? Well, I am here to tell you that it is you and you alone. Strive to form positive thoughts in your head and in your heart whenever you walk on the court.

The fiercest opponent you will ever face in tennis is a "bad attitude." Tremendous abilities can be wasted when a bad attitude sets in. It can block out your desire to learn, destroy your ability to concentrate, and slowly break down your self-control. You could even say that your tennis future hangs in the balance when a poor attitude creeps into the picture. Think discouraging thoughts, and you will be a discouraged player. Think encouraging thoughts, and you will be an encouraged and

motivated player. What you think about most often will form your attitude.

So control your thoughts in order to develop and maintain a positive attitude.

A winning attitude does not mean you should become obsessed with winning. You should strive for your best effort and regularly play up to your best potential. You should channel all of your energies and determination into being the best you can be. Many of the top players try to raise the level of their games with a little fist pump after winning an important point. It can work for you, too.

3 learn to relax

Have you ever been nervous enough to worry about an upcoming match? Have you ever been so nervous that the game seemed more difficult than it did when you practiced? One way to improve your performance when your mind seems to be full of worry is simply to relax. You do not want to relax your mind, just the muscles in your body. You will find that most of your worries will stop once your body becomes truly relaxed on court.

The important thing to remember about relaxing is never to force it. It will never come about by trying hard to relax. Chances are you only will create more worry and tension for yourself by thinking so hard about it. It must come effortlessly and easily, or it will not come at all.

When the score is close, inexperienced players tend to feel pressure as negative thoughts enter the mind. Anxiety, fear, frustration, and temper can tighten the muscles in your body and hinder your play. On the other hand, positive thoughts calm the mind, allowing you to concentrate better.

Do your best to think positively about your performance under all game situations. Failure to do this can cause you to choke when you need to play your best. Choking is what athletes call "fear of failure." When a player chokes during a match and misses a shot, the muscles in the body are tense, the heart is racing, and the player feels clammy, maybe even nauseated. This happens because anxiety is present in the mind.

The first thing you should do if you ever find yourself choking is to slow down. Slow down your breathing, slow down your walk, and, most of all, slow down your tendency to play fast. Take more time between points. Attempt to clear your mind of all unwanted thoughts. Take a deep breath and recommit your thoughts to the challenge of the match. Long, deep, slow breathing can send a message to the mind, telling it that the body is relaxed and back in control. Karate students are taught to exhale when they chop or punch. This helps them to relax their muscles for more control and power on contact. It can work for tennis players, too.

4 develop a routine

One of the most common phrases yelled out on a tennis court is "Watch the ball!" This is often the comment of a player attempting to focus the mind and concentrate on the match, not necessarily because the player is not keeping an eye on the ball. However, it is true that controlling your eyes on a tennis court can help you control your mind. Allowing your eyes to drift can cause your mind to drift. Simply put, there are just too many distractions that can take away your focus. The more your vision is focused, the more your mind is focused on the task at hand.

Concentration is the ability to focus on the moment. It is the ability to block or control the internal and external distractions. Players who concentrate well can forget about bad shots they have made in the past, and they have confidence in their ability to pull off good shots in the future. Ideally, your focus is on the ball, the point, the match, and the moment. Concentration is a skill that can be developed through practice. Once you learn to focus your mind, your attention and concentration then becomes more controlled.

Many experienced players develop routines to help them concentrate. For example, some players bounce the ball several times as they prepare to serve, some players avoid making eye contact with their opponents by turning their backs to them as they prepare their minds for returning serve, and some simply walk around behind the baseline to gather their thoughts. The specific behavior makes no difference; do whatever it takes to hold your concentration.

Sometimes players lose their concentration between points by allowing their eyes to wander. Control your concentration by focusing on your racquet at the conclusion of each point. Adjust your strings or simply look at your racquet so that your mind remains on the match.

5 change the way you think

Confidence is seeing what you want to happen rather than what might happen. Confident tennis players feel good about themselves even when not playing their best. They have a clear image of their abilities and believe in them.

Self-confidence can be developed through a conditioning process of practice and belief. It requires positive habits of thought in your mind and in your actions. Learn to "think like a winner." Visualize and think positive thoughts about what you would like to happen, and block out doubtful thoughts on things that have yet to occur.

Many young players have trouble believing in themselves and their abilities. The problem is that when they place themselves at a particular level of play, they will usually remain there until they change the way they think of themselves. To get to next level of play, etch a confident image of your tennis abilities into your mind. Regard yourself and your abilities in terms of your strengths. Do not forget your weaknesses when it is time to improve them, but do not measure your tennis game strictly by them.

Winners believe they will win. They believe until the final point of the match has been played. If they find themselves behind in a match, they have the ability to surge ahead through strong conviction and belief in themselves as well as determination not to accept defeat.

6 commit to get to every ball

Like many other teaching pros, when I look for a youngster's potential talent in tennis, I look for three things: the desire to win, a good attitude, and—most important—good footwork.

Footwork is important because your feet line you up for contact with the ball. It is just that simple. The pros make the game look so easy because their footwork is so very good. They line up correctly for each shot without having to make uncoordinated body moves and stabs at the ball, like many lower level players do. They understand the importance of good footwork and let their feet do the work in bringing out successful play in themselves. They are able to "groove their strokes," hitting similar shots over and over again, by lining up the ideal position to play each shot.

If you wish to advance your game, you should make a commitment to reach all balls on court. Your capacity to reach just one extra ball and send it back across the net could raise your game another notch. This may require you to get in shape, because when you commit to reach all balls on court, you must be prepared to keep this up for an entire match.

The first thing you can usually look for when stroking problems develop is slow moving feet. This is why so many professionals of the game train so hard to keep their tennis play at the highest level. They, too, have made a commitment to reach all balls on court and fully intend to uphold this commitment, no matter how many miles they have to run during the match they play.

practice properly

Playing tennis is so much fun that many players seem reluctant to practice it. That is a mistake, of course, because practice is the best way to use your time if you are serious about raising the level of your game. In a properly organized practice session, you will hit many more balls than you would in a couple of sets of match play. In fact, do you know who practices the most? Tennis professionals. The pros know that they have to work to keep their game at a high level and that practice is the best way to ensure that.

Winning is a challenging and demanding for the average junior as well as the professional. But success doesn't come cheap. Sure, some players are born with certain physical attributes that give them an edge in becoming better players. But for the rest of us, how do we get to the next level?

Your local tournament can mean as much to you as winning one of the grand slam tournaments means to a professional. Successful training habits are essential in reaching the next level of play. Preparation through practice techniques and proper training is the way to go. For that reason, it is important to consider some practice and training habits that work for the pros. They will also work for you, the developing junior.

1 warm up before you practice

If you practice properly, you will be working hard—perhaps harder than you do in a match. That is because you will hit more balls and do more running to keep balls in play than you would in competition.

Because of that, you should warm up carefully before your practice session. Start with some easy stretching exercises. Begin by loosening your neck muscles and then move down to your arms, upper body, and legs until you have stretched every muscle that you use when playing. Make sure you are physically warm before you start hitting balls. That's especially important during the cooler months, but make every effort to warm up every time you go out on the court.

2 start out slowly

After stretching exercises, begin your on-court practice by hitting easy balls for a few minutes. If you and your practice partner have good forehands, hit some forehands to each other. However, do not demonstrate your prowess by hitting winners; simply try to keep the rally going.

As you warm up, gradually increase the depth and pace of your balls and begin hitting to both sides. Start to hit wider balls, so you both have to run to make your returns.

When you are hitting easily, move up to the net and hit a few volleys. Get your partner to hit you some easy balls, then some low ones. Then do the same for your partner.

Finally, finish off with a few unhurried serves and some lobs that can be smashed without difficulty. Do it all at a relatively slow pace so you are thoroughly warmed up and can hit with consistency and confidence. After that, you can get down to the real business of practicing.

3 be goal oriented

When was the last time you walked onto a tennis court just to hit a few balls with a friend or practice partner without having a specific purpose in mind? To make the most of your court time, use your practice time wisely. You would do well to remember this very important point: "Aimless hitting produces aimless play." Balls that are directed all over the court without target areas and ball placement in mind are really just uncontrollable shots being practiced.

To make matters worse, the mind is not used in this form of practice either. When players choose to practice this way, just going through the motions of ball-striking aimlessly, they are really developing a recipe for disaster.

Focused players are usually driven by thoughts of reaching personal goals. They know what it is they are going after and channel all their energies into attaining those goals. You probably won't see these players hitting aimlessly or mindlessly because they are tuned in each time they walk on court. Their mission is to improve their games, and they realize that in order to do that, they must use their practice time to develop and improve their play. They are motivated and disciplined because they have become goal-orientated.

All tennis players, from the beginner to the advanced player, needs goals. Obviously the goals or aspirations of the players will vary with each level and individual, but it is important that each player sets a direction.

When setting goals, remember that they must be specific, realistic, and, above all, attainable. For example, if your ultimate goal is to play college tennis, set short-term and medium-range goals along the way to ensure success. Your short-term goals will provide the initial steps required to take you where you want to go with your tennis game. As a high school student, I set an ultimate goal of making a college tennis team. My short-term goals were to practice daily with specific improvements in mind. My medium-range goals were to make the high school team and to enter as many summer tournaments as I could. Once I accomplished those goals, I began to have a better idea of what it would take to play at the college level.

To achieve your ultimate goal, try to remember that practice should be fun, exciting, and challenging. Setting and accomplishing short-term and medium-range goals can help you keep your interest level high as you work toward reaching your ultimate goal.

4 drill for consistency

Reaching your best playing level requires consistency of play. To aim for consistent results with your game, begin by establishing consistent habits. Players who play the game within themselves, that is, the game of which they know they are capable, develop strokes they can count on in practice. You will not see them hitting shots with a low percentage chance of success, because they have built their games on reliable strokes that are consistently played.

Drilling is an ideal way to "groove" strokes—to make them consistent and develop your confidence in them. Many young

players avoid dull drill practice in favor of the excitement of point playing. While match play and point play are also important, nothing develops your game's consistency more than establishing good practice patterns and habits, which includes drilling.

There are hundreds of drills that can be used. Your local teaching professional can help you choose which drills would be best suited for your particular needs and game. Collect a supply of tennis balls and search for a practice partner who will not be bored drilling with you. The skill level of your partner should not matter. It is not important who is on the court with you; your aim is to play your best, no matter who is on the other side of the net.

5 time well spent

The time you spend on the court honing your game should be time well spent. Since you are developing either good or bad habits each time you walk on the court, it is of utmost importance that you give your all every time you pick up a racquet. You should never practice unless you feel like it. If you get used to playing when you really do not have the desire, you will develop the bad habit of playing the game with less intensity, and you get used to playing that way. It is much better to practice only when you can commit to giving your all.

Possessing a genuine desire to improve will help you reach your best more often. Just showing up, going through the motions, and putting in your court time will not guarantee success. In other words, it is not the time you put in that counts, it is the effort during that time.

For example, when was the last time you let the ball bounce twice on your side of the net while playing a match? You probably gave it your all to run it down before the second bounce. Have you always given the same concern for double bounces during practice? You should. The way you practice is the way you play.

Your concentration, intensity, total effort, and desire are all determining factors in developing your game and your strokes, turning you into a unique player. Since most of your tennis time probably is spent on the practice court, it is imperative that you learn to practice the way you would like to play. When you learn to do that, then and only then, will you have spent your time well.

6 practice your weaknesses

When you are well into your practice session, you should work on your weaknesses. Spend at least ten minutes on a single shot. You'll be amazed at the number of balls you can hit in that amount of time. And you will be equally surprised by the improvement of your shot after that amount of concentrated hitting.

Suppose low volleys are giving you trouble. Stand back on the service line and have your practice partner send balls to you low over the net. Hit every ball before it bounces, but move back to the service line after each one. That way, all the balls you hit will be low volleys. But remember, your main objective is to clear the net with depth, not to hit a winner. Even the pros have trouble volleying winners off a low hit ball, so just concentrate on getting the ball back over the net.

7 a time to experiment

While I have stressed the importance of consistency when you practice, I do not want you to get the idea that you should be conservative. Your practice sessions should also be a time to experiment, to try to develop a new shot.

Push yourself to the limits as you practice. You can do this by playing every ball that passes over the net. For example, even if your partner's lob is going out, smash it back by making that extra effort. Similarly, get your partner to blast a few serves at you and try to return any that clear the net, even if they land outside the service box. Then, the next time you face a hard serving player in a match, you will have your swing grooved and ready for action.

W hen your strokes feel good in practice, test them by taking the ball a little earlier. By testing yourself in practice, you will find that you can do more than you had thought possible.

glossary of tennis terms

adjustment steps – positioning of the feet taken while preparing to take a forward swing at the ball or when establishing a hitting stance

approach shot – a ground stroke hit from inside the baseline in order to get to the net to make an offensive stand

backhand – a primary shot executed with the racquet arm in front of you when in a hitting stance

backswing – the initial movement of bringing your racquet behind you before you begin your forward swing

baseline – the line at the back of the court that runs parallel to the net

choking – fear of failure and the inability to perform well in certain circumstances

concentration – the ability to focus on the moment, blocking or controlling internal and external distractions

confidence – believing in yourself; focusing on what you want to happen rather than what might happen

crossover steps – running while remaining predominately parallel to the net, overlapping your legs and feet efficiently

drilling – specific practicing designed to improve a specific stroke or pattern of play

drop shot – a softly hit shot landing very short in your opponents court to gain an offensive position

follow-through – the completion of your swing that gives you more control over your shot

forehand – a primary shot executed with the racquet arm behind you when in a hitting stance

footwork – the adjustments made with your feet when getting into position to swing at the ball

ground stroke – a forehand or backhand usually hit from the backcourt after the ball bounces

half-volley – a shot hit in a volley-like manner after the ball bounces

hitting stance – a solid foundation or position assumed when setting up for a ground stroke

lob – a shot hit with a relatively high trajectory, landing deep in your opponent's court

movement – the act of getting from one area of the court to the other quickly and efficiently

overhead smash – an offensive shot you hit when the ball is over your head in an attempt to end the point

ready stance – the positioning and posture you assume when preparing to move or hit the ball

serve – a shot hit to begin each point

shuffle-steps – adjustment of the feet in gaining a better court position while remaining predominately parallel to the net

slice (or underspin) – action applied to the ball created by brushing down the backside of the ball with a high to low swing pattern, keeping the ball low to the court

split-step – a little hop you take just before your opponent hits the ball, enabling you to move in any direction efficiently

swing pattern – the angle of approach to impact with your racquet from backswing to follow-through

topspin – action applied to the ball created by brushing up the backside of the ball with a low to high swing pattern, giving your shot more net clearance